FUMBLING TO FLUENCY

A READING JOURNEY

SIDDHI SANGRAM LIMAYE

This book is dedicated to anyone who struggles with reading and wishes to change it in near future. This book is also dedicated to voracious readers, who can look back into their past and relate at some point!

Contents

Foreword

An extremely interesting read, not just for younger audiences but for anyone in general, who relates to the struggle of learning to read and appreciate books. The story about the author is quite a challenging one, and knowing that l myself have played a key influence in her adventure does no more than delight to me.

- Swayam Pathak

Tokyo, Japan

Preface

Hi Siddhi here, I welcome you aboard on the adventure of my reading journey. It may be my reading journey, but I am sure that you will relate to it at some point!

My story starts about 9 years ago, just when parents start comparing and making their expectations list, which is seemingly endless.... I was 4 at that time, as innocent as kids are, and newly introduced to the world of schooling and competition. Well, what are kindergarten kids expected to do? Learn letters, learn numbers and eventually learn to read. Here's the plot twist, I simply couldn't read. While my cousins were reading perfectly well at the age of 6, I couldn't till the age of 11.

As they say, 'change is the only constant thing'. My story couldn't remain same forever. It had to take turns, and it did!

My reading journey has been really adventurous and funny. It often brought anger, sobbing, embarrassment and of course comparison. I thought why not share this story with you guys. There have been lots of heart breaking incidents but I have decided to include a few of them.

Acknowledgements

I take privilege in writing this acknowledgement!

Firstly I would thank Mrs. Himani Ved, for investing her precious time into this little project. She is the charm giver to this book. Her editing skills are unbeatable! I must say she has poured her heart into it.

My big thanks to Mrs. Ketaki Bankapure for writing, author's introduction. She has written wonderfully about a topic which wasn't so profound!

I thank, Master Swayam Pathak (my cousin) for writing the forward of this book. He did it on a short notice this which is even more appreciable.

I will take a movement to thank Dr. Mamata Limaye (my mother) for spending hours in the tedious publication process. She is the back bone of the project!

Next I would love to thank my family, for encouraging me to write this book. This was impossible without their support and suggestions!

I would also express my gratitude towards my school Canossa Convent High School, Dhule for arranging different competitions time to time, so that more people like me can get a chance to improve themselves.

Last but not the least I would thank all the people who have been part of my reading journey. Positive or negative, each experience has taught me something or the other which will always stay with me.

CHAPTER ONE

Surprise tests, which happened too often!

I enjoy going shopping with my mother but that didn't necessarily mean travelling to the shops had to be good enough. We often came across posters and commercials written in either Marathi, Hindi or English. My mother was so desperate to make me read that she never left a single chance to do so.

I sat behind my mother on a moped, wondering how I would spend the evening. My mother always loves starting conversations in a soft and loving tone. (Let's ignore the fact that this leads to yelling at me in the end or giving me the special looks that my mother has mastered through the years).

So even that day she started the conversation saying "*Manu te bagh*"(Dear look at that). I didn't need to look up to know what she was pointing at. It had to be a written text which she hoped I could read. As I expected it was a hoarding. My mother continued "*vach tar te bara*"(Give it a try). I was in such a dilemma and read aloud the letters "K-A-N-A-L M-E-N-S W-E-A-R *kanal te madhala nahi vachata yet ani last cha tear*"(Kanal I can't read the middle word and last one is tear). My mother shouted at me " *Murkha...*

*te Kamal mens wear aahe ani shevatchaya shabbat T kuthe distoy tare vachayala ... huh?". (F*ool! It's kamal mens wear and where do you see T in the last word to read it as tear, huh?). She held my hand and dragged me away being very disappointed with my progress. Well, saying progress might be a little inappropriate, because I never made any progress.

This wasn't the first or last such incident, making my mother more and more tensed about my future. I could see the worry in her eyes and I thought to myself, how dumb am I? I can't even read!!!

CHAPTER TWO

Why can't the waiter read out the whole menu to us?

During winter holidays, the whole family gathered together planning to go for lunch. Sounds wonderful, doesn't it? We went for lunch as decided to one of our favorite restaurants of all times, 'Krishnai'.

Everyone rushed to the car and started proposing different ideas about what to order. Even I suggested some dishes. When we actually reached the restaurant and booked a perfect table for our family, in front of me came the menu card. Anyone reading this would obviously question that isn't this very normal when you go to a restaurant. Well apparently not for me. I absolutely didn't have any problem with the content on the card, but reading the content was my real concern.

When families gather and everyone's in a good mood, of course kids are indulged. As were we, my cousins and I. Everyone encouraged us to suggest something on the menu. I was delighted! My eyes ran through the menu but indeed I was ignorant, ignorant to anything related to alphabets. Meaning, I couldn't read! I tried my hardest, breaking the words trying to pronounce it and letting it come together, but in the end that didn't make any sense. While I was breaking words, others had finished ordering. In order to get out of the situation I pushed the menu card away, and said "anything will do for me". Deep down I wanted to choose something, but couldn't. Anyways asking someone else to read it out for me was too embarrassing to imagine.

This is when I first realized, that if I wanted to live happily, I must be able to read.

CHAPTER THREE

Fruits turned out to be bitter.

This is a very small incident, but it contributed a lot to my realization process. I was sitting with a few of my friends. We were making a list of fruits for some sort of game. I am absolutely not sure in what state of mind I was at the time, I got the pen and paper and took the responsibility of making the list. Somebody said, “Apple” others said “Orange”,” mango” voices behind me said, “banana”, ”grapes”, “strawberry”. I was confused, but with all my courage, the nib of my pen touched the paper. I choose Apple to be first on the list. I was sure Apple started with an ‘A’. I quickly wrote ‘A’ but what next?! I was blank somebody volunteered ‘P’. Again I wrote that down and before I could realize, one of my friends snatched the pen and paper from my hand and exclaimed, “Do you even know to write?”.

The chaos of my friends didn’t matter to me anymore. It dawned upon me, if I cannot read I cannot write.

Even though I went to one of the top schools in my city that is ‘Canossa Convent High School’, my teachers never realized my inefficiency with reading because I had memorized all my text books in fear of embarrassment. I was very young, so I had limited academic syllabus, that's why memorizing it was possible. Due to my stubbornness to avoid embarrassment, my teachers never recognized the situation hence they couldn't help me either.

At this point I was totally convinced that I must to something to gain reading ability. What 'something' was the question. Let's move on to the next incidents.

CHAPTER FOUR

Memorizing under the name of phonics scam!

My life has never been less than a roller coaster and you will soon know why. My mother had finally found that something to fill in the gap of my reading journey. It was one of the most popular places in my little town, Dhule, known for its variety of courses including phonics.

To be frank it was a bleak, dull and gray sort of place where I was nervous to step in. Somewhat hiding behind my mother I entered the room. After some casual conversation, my mother introduced me. I was continuously shifting my weight from one foot to the other and glanced around the room trying to avoid eye contact with the person sitting on the chair in front of me. He asked me a few questions, which I barely answered, and assured by mother that she had nothing to worry about. I can say it was my mother's second very last hope. From this statement you might have guessed, that this venture, although was promising in the beginning was unsuccessful.

Next day my mother dropped me to the mind-numbing place, which was nothing more than a normal classroom filled with kids. A tedious story in short, all I did there was literally learned spellings and not phonics. They made us memorize the most common spellings which we often see around.

Let me be straight forward, I couldn't read but my IQ was decent. I was doing a good job memorizing tons of spelling, and then pretending to read and write. Passing my mother's surprise tests had become a piece of cake, which give her immense pleasure. All this bliss came under false pretences. After 6 months, that's the completion of the course we were called and tested in front of all parents. I honestly don't know what the purpose of this exercise was. It made my all knowing mother understand the entire, memorizing under the name of teaching phonics, scam. The perception, that I was learning a lot, which she had held in her mind for 6 months was pricked like a balloon.

Now look, I wasn't that matured to understand this entire scenario. At that time, all I cared about was my mother being satisfied. The previous 6 months had been great, but now they were about to take a turn for the worse. I could see that my mother was dejected. We left that place once and for all. This time my mother said nothing so naturally I was silent too.

CHAPTER FIVE

When my mother took matters in her hand....

As I mentioned my days were about to get worst. So the time had come. My mother concluded that no one could influence my reading journey except her.

Immediately, the day after the phonics disaster, I found my mother at the book shelf deciding my fate. She was keenly choosing a book for me. I couldn't bear this sight anymore so I ran away.

That same evening we were sitting at the dining table. I had forgotten about the horror I experienced in the morning and I was delightfully enjoying my evening snacks. At a leisurely pace, my mother slid the book in front of me. At the sight of the book, I choked on the biscuits in my mouth. My mother didn't need to say anything. I knew what I was supposed to do. With all my courage, I gently opened the first page of the book that read 'Story of the frog'. Before starting the battle of reading, with my neck down I just raised my pupils and stared at my downcast mother, but her sight was focused on the book. My eyes returned to the words and me and my mother shared eye gaze.

As expected I took almost 20 to 30 minutes to read a page. PHONICS for sure was showing its results! The page barely consisted 7 to 8 lines in big font. After spending almost a month of afternoons and some evenings we completed the first book.

At the same pace, I read another 2 to 3 books. Although I might have made 0.0001% progress it was too little to satisfy anyone. I would often read something wrong then my mother would shout and get irritated. Social embarrassments continued unabated. My mother's distress increased with time.

Prior to moving on to the next chapter let me tell you something about reading. Being able to read and loving reading are immensely different. With my mother's unstoppable efforts I could even read to some extent, but you know the inner desire to read is what makes you fall in love with reading. Everyone has different ways of igniting their desire. Some may start reading to learn something new and then end up in love with reading. For others, the pleasure of reading would be rewarding. In my case it was 'Harry Potter' about which you will soon know in detail.

CHAPTER SIX

Ray of hope strikes.

This time my mother came up with a completely new plan. She thought of showing me English movies with subtitles so that at least for the sake of understanding the story I would pay attention to the words. Another reason was to improve my vocabulary and sentence framing, as my spoken English was no better.

We started with 'Kung Fu Panda' then 'Harry Potter'. I must say this plan was much better than previous ways of harassing me and yes I was paying some attention to the subtitles.

Eventually I started reading books. To encourage me further, my mother made Book titled 'Siddhi's reading journey'. Each book read by me would be entered in it with the name of the author and number of pages in the book. That inspired me to read bigger books. So at this point you can say that I could read but definitely needed to polish it a lot and loving reading was still a different story.

Well, have you guys realized the timeline of my story? That is my age till the previous incident. At the start I was around 9 years old and by the end of it I was 11 years old. Things didn't improve much in those years, but they were about to.

CHAPTER SEVEN

Oceans apart.

In a random afternoon call with my aunt, the conversation landed on the topic 'Siddhi staying at aunt's place for summer'. At the start I honestly thought that these adults were just day dreaming about the whole thing, but I was wrong. 5 to 10 minutes into the call everyone sounded serious about it. My uncle had started checking the tickets and they had already started making plans for my stay.

You might think what is the big deal about visiting your aunt? Let me tell you, my aunt lives in Japan and I was going there all by myself at the age of 11. Exciting, isn't it!

Within a couple of days, my tickets for Japan were booked and I was ready to fly both literally and in my reading journey. I was staying there for one month. My mother, grandparents and me, we will cool about it but my father was a little worried because Japan was 5956 km from India and if I missed my parents there was no way back! Overall everyone was happy. A lot was waiting for me in foreign lands.

As the proverb goes, 'if you are best in the classroom you are in the wrong classroom'. I wasn't the best or anything but as I mentioned earlier that even though I couldn't read much my IQ wasn't low. So I was doing good at academics. I lived in a small town and it's not like we are any less talented but sometime we lack the exposure to the outer world and to the opportunities it holds. We might seem to be good in our own skin but lacked the confidence and boldness which kids with exposure had in spades. In my case with limited ability to read my confidence was already blown away even before it was built. Now you get the idea and background for how important this trip was.

CHAPTER EIGHT

Ready to fly.

My parents dropped me at Mumbai International Airport. I was accompanied on the flight by family friends of my aunt, whom I met for the first time at the airport. So kind of like strangers but still you can say that I was accompanied.

I had to wave goodbye to my parents outside the airport. I stepped inside with all my courage, carrying my luggage. Taking a deep breath, I went through the immigration process. I was asked a few more and special questions because seldom you will find a 11 year old traveling alone. The questions were like; if I was travelling of my own free will, if my parents had no objection to it, what was my purpose of going to Japan, what do I do in India, which is my school and so on.

After the immigration process we sat at the departure area where I was collecting my thoughts and I remembered how I had prepared for coming to Japan. It started with learning the language. I had installed a language learning app called 'Duolingo' from which I learned basic Japanese and I learned Japanese through English so it helped me prepare in that way too.

At this point, I was so desperate to do something with my reading that there was no looking back. For the first time I cared as much as my mother. I had become so engrossed in thinking about it that nothing seemed more important to me. I was so busy pondering my decisions that I didn't realize how time had passed.

I was brought back to reality by my guardians for that day. We stepped in the plane, I found my seat and sat there apprehensive about leaving my parents. The plane soared high in sky and so did my thoughts. After a few minutes the plane wasn't ascending anymore, it was stable and so was my anxiety. I stopped worrying about what awaited me, probably because there was no other option. I thought positively that I may be going to a strange land but I wasn't meeting strangers. I was going to my aunt and I also had my cousin and uncle there. My aunt's mother-in-law and father-in-law were also visiting them at the same time so that was a plus point too.

After a long flight of 10 hours, the wheels of the plane touched the remarkable and unforgettable land of Japan.

CHAPTER NINE

The night lamp created the spark.

After such a long flight I felt a little sore and dizzy. We came out of the airport after an hour so. My aunt and uncle had come to pick me up. We loaded my luggage and I waved and thanked my guardians for the day.

I was very happy to meet my aunt and uncle. We had a lovely conversation on the way from the airport to home. The journey was about one and half hours. After the ocean of excitement had settled by talking we were quiet for sometime. I was quiet physically, but inside I was bubbling with enthusiasm. I didn't leave a single chance to observe from the rectangular car window. What an extraordinary country Japan was! I must say this was one of the most exciting hour of my life. This place was just giving me so much inspiration and finally it was happening I was interested in inspiring myself.

I settled down very quickly. I unpacked my bag, arranged my clothes in the closet and waited until my brother returned from school.

I don't recollect from where this idea came but I remember watching first part of 'Harry Potter' that is 'Philosopher's stone'. I had found it very interesting but due to my lack of fluency in English. I wasn't able to understand the story as a whole. I also knew that the movies were made from books and felt that if I read the books I would be able to understand the plot. Before my inspiration died, I quickly asked my aunt for the 'Harry Potter' books. I was sure they would have the books because my brother read a lot. As expected she handed the books over to me, but for the first time somebody told me not to read and sleep first so that I wouldn't suffer from jet lag.

I was told to sleep until lunch time but my curiosity lured me into opening the first book. I flipped through it. Carrying a book as big as that made me feel proud. Since my capacity to deal with words was very limited shuffling through pages resulted into a nap even before I knew it.

That same evening I went to play at a park nearby with my cousin and his friends. It was very refreshing. After dinner we chilled out for some time and then me and my cousin started preparing for bed. It was very generous of him to let me sleep on the bed and he slept on the floor. That was one of the most warmth giving things in Japan.

By the way my brother's name is Swayam. So Swayam had a beautiful and definitely way more organized bedroom than me. It had wide windows, a small balcony, a closet, a study table, a single bed. The back of the bed had a wider top so over it was situated a reading lamp, because he read a lot. I was very eager to use that reading lamp that night.

After my aunt kissed us good night and switch off the lights. I switched on the reading light and open the first 'Harry Potter' book. My eyes ran through the words and this time I did not deter. I read a few pages may it be slow, may it wrong but still I kept on reading. Probably, because there was no one to judge me. After an hour my eyes felt stressed and I closed the book.

Congratulations to the readers the long awaited moment had come. It was for the first time I had read for so long with my own interest. That night I had a sense of satisfaction. It wasn't just about reading. It was about all the decisions that me and my family had made that help me reach Japan.

My stay there was a lot of fun. In the morning Swayam would go to school and me, my aunt and grandparents that is my aunt's mother-in-law and father-in- law could go out and explore. In the evenings Swayam, his friends and I would go to play at a park. At night I used to switch on the reading lamp and open the book and read.

Surprisingly my reading was improving, the amount of time I read also increased. In a short period of 1 month I reached to a point that I used to continuously read for 3 to 4 hours at night. Definitely my mother had a lion's share in it but I mean come on J.K. Rowling the author of 'Harry Potter' her writing is so fabulous that even a critic of any kind won't be able to put the book down. My vocabulary was increasing and my confidence was increasing as well. Reading helped my spoken English too. When I went out with people of my age previously I used to feel very self conscious, but with all those improvements it had started to vanish. In some casual phone calls, my aunt used to tell my mother that I had made a lot of improvements because my case was well known across my family. My mother could not believe it for obvious reasons, what had not been achieved forcefully was happening by my own will. I used to call my family daily. I had so much tell about my enjoyment in Japan that the topic never landed on my reading. One night I was talking to my mother we both had a lot of free time on our hands. I don't need to tell what happens when mother and daughter are free, but still for those who don't know, they talk a lot. After chatting for some time. I started telling her about 'Harry Potter'. I told her about how I read a lot, and how interesting the story is. I also told her that I had finished to 2 books from 'Harry Potter' series and I would be starting the third book. At the same time she promised me that she would buy me Harry Potter books when I returned to India. What a heart to heart conversation it was. For the first time me and my mother, were happily talking about reading.

Actually I had so many wonderful experiences in Japan, that this little episode isn't enough. Rather it deserves a completely separate book. I have only focused about reading in Japan in this book.

CHAPTER TEN

Words acted as magic.

My stay in Japan was coming to an end. We started packing all my things. I was a little sad about leaving Japan but at the same time I was excited to come back to my homeland. I had my flight in the morning at around 8:00 a.m.. This time too I was accompanied by my aunt's family friend. After bidding a heartfelt goodbye to my aunt and her family, we boarded the plane. This time there was no anxiety, no nervousness just excitement.

Usually, flights are boring but I was determined to not let it happen on this particular journey. I had been curious about various things since childhood, but due to lack of confidence I was afraid to ask questions. So I ended up suppressing my curiosity and everybody had concluded that I lacked curiosity. With my new found ability to read, in a way I was proving wrong every single individual, who had ever had the faintest thought that I was dumb.

After watching a Disney movie, I thought of stretching my limits and trying to convert my reading enthusiasm into going out and talking to people. I always wanted to know how the crew onboard functioned. So I was continuously trying to peep into their kitchen but failed to even get a glance of it. Being frustrated, I got up and without giving it a second thought I was literally standing outside the kitchen of my plane and sliding the curtain a bit with my hand. It was sort of a break time for the air hostesses so nobody was working and they were fixing their makeup. Initially they thought that I was there to ask for something, so one of them asked in a soothing tone, "do you need anything child". That's when I realized that I had landed myself into a little difficult situation, I had to speak in English. I took a deep and said, "no thanks! Actually, I wanted to know how you guys worked. If you don't mind showing me around, will you?" one of them said, "why not". Everybody introduced themselves to me and showed me around the kitchen, which was nothing more than piles of ready to eat food and a dozen microwaves. Later on they asked for my personal details and they were also surprised by the fact that I was travelling alone. They asked about India as well and I was delighted to fill them in. After this conversation I decided to leave. On the note of saying goodbye, I complimented them that I really liked their makeup and the scarf they wore around their neck, which was part of their uniform. I don't know if they were in love with India or me, but they decided to give me some makeup and tie the scarf around my neck. After receiving this hospitable treatment, I was so happy that all my nervousness had flown away. I must say these beautiful Japanese ladies made my day! For rest of the 5 hours of the flight I received VIP treatment which overwhelmed me.

This incident taught me that there is nothing to be afraid to go out and talk to people. Nobody judges you as much as you think and even if they do it should not affect you. I know it's not related to reading but it has emerged through reading and that's why I think it has a place in this book.

CHAPTER ELEVEN

A shock on the dining table.

The flight landed and I couldn't wait another second to meet my family. My mother had come to pick me up from the airport. She was eagerly waiting outside the arrival gate. As time passed, our hearts raced faster, impatient to meet each other. Finally my eyes found her through the crowd and I carelessly left my luggage and ran to hug her. I stayed in her arms for a minute, realizing how much I had missed her. My grandfather's brother and his wife had also come to receive me as they lived not too far from the airport. Their presence was a pleasant surprise.

Apart from this I was a little disappointed, that my father hadn't come but I preferred not to mention it. After traveling for half an hour, the car stopped outside a commercial looking building. I naturally questioned my mother about it. She said that someone was coming. Usually my parents tell me everything so this little answer didn't satisfy me. Before I could grasp the situation I saw my father waiting outside the car. I can't explain how happy I was at seeing him! I opened the door and hugged him tight. Later they explained, that he had had a meeting to attend and couldn't finish it in time so they planed the surprise. For the journey of the next 6 hours, from Mumbai to Dhule, I was continuously talking.

We reached Dhule around midnight. The next morning I did something very unexpected. Before unpacking my bag or talking about shopping, I asked for the next 'Harry Potter' books on the dining table itself. This is a little dramatic but true. Everybody was engaged with their own tasks. On hearing my demand my parents and grandparents left all their work and came and sat on the dining table. Dear readers, image how happy my mother must have been. Then and there we ordered the set of 7 books.

They arrived after three days and until then I was restless. Once they arrived they were handed over to me. I read day and night. I didn't even leave the books while eating. In this manner I finished the first five books of 'Harry Potter' ranging from 200 pages to 700 pages in extremely tiny font. My family's deepest desires were finally being fulfilled. I decided to continue maintaining the diary of list of books read by me, which was an initiative made by my mother to encourage me as I had mentioned earlier.

By then my school had already started so I got time to read only at night. That too, maximum for an hour and a half. Reading become a part of my daily routine.

Around the same time, my school organized a wonderful initiative of reading. Something other than text books, i.e. In the last half hour of school, we were encouraged to read small story books which could be finished in half an hour. Due to this many students at least came in touch with reading.

Everybody had started to notice changes in fluency in my language. They also took note of my newly found self confidence.

Now it might seem that the story has come to an end but still I had to nail a few things.

CHAPTER TWELVE

When I was declared an owl.

My aunt came to know that I was having a hard time with reading because I didn't get time to read. Listening to this she said that she would do something, but I wondered what.

She was visiting India around the time of Raksha Bandhan that is in August. After many years my father and my aunt and me and my brother were celebrating Raksha Bandhan together. After the rituals, when it was time for exchanging gifts my brother told me to close my eyes and placed in my hands a thin, rectangular, solid, 15 x 10 cm gadget. To my astonishment it was a 'Kindle'!

For those who don't know what Kindle is, it's a fantasy for anyone who loves reading. Basically 'Kindle' is the series of e-readers designed and marketed by Amazon. You can browse, buy, download and read books and other digital media via wireless networking to the 'Kindle' Store. Do not let this illusion fool you that Kindle is something similar to a tablet. Kindle's interface is completely different. The technology used in it is not even close to a normal screen. The screen of Kindle is comparatively very less harmful to eyes, I can say almost unharmful and you can't do anything in it except read.

So coming back to the incident, I was flattered by this innovative gift. My aunt said that I can read with Kindle at night even when lights are turned off without spoiling my eyes. It was so good of my brother to preload hundreds of books on the Kindle before gifting it to me. However the 'Kindle' had adverse effects on me. It was expected that I would read at night for an hour, but I used to get so engrossed into the books that I used to read until 1 or 2 p.m. at night, which is quite an unhealthy habit. So whenever my parents used to wake up they saw a faint white light in the pitch dark room and ended up calling me an owl.

It was nice for a few days for me and my parents but no matter when I slept I had to wake up at 6:00 a.m. for school. So my parents, told me to stop reading at night and sleep on time. I somehow couldn't stop my addiction to reading and continued it. Probably it happened because I had struggled so much with it and now that I was being able to read, I wanted to do it more than ever.

My family decided that they would snatch away the 'Kindle' from me at night and they did so. Can you imagine over a few pages how the dice had turned. From being forced into reading I was being deprived from it. By now I had finished the entire Harry Potter series and few other books too.

CHAPTER THIRTEEN

Shalaka- Enlightening minds.

Around November in my 6 grade I enrolled to participate in a workshop 'Kathamancha' conducted by an organization called 'Shalaka'. It aimed at all round development of children. It was owned by a psychologist, Mrs. Ketaki Mhaskar Bankapure. She is like a sister to me and also our closest neighbor both in terms of distance and relation. The ambitions for 'Kathamancha' are the same as this book, that's establishing reading habits.

It was a very nice set up with hundreds of books to choose from. Those who were good at reading could find their perfect corner and continue reading there. I got in touch with many versatile books there. We could also interact with other readers which helped our communication skills. For those who could not read, people at 'Shalaka' taught them to do so.

At the end of each session, we would brief each other about the knowledge we had gained on that day. Here I realized how far I had come. I stood out amongst other children. My language was fluent, I had knowledge about comparatively more things and I understood the power of reading. This further improved my confidence.

So thank you ‘Shalaka’, for organizing such enriching workshop.

CHAPTER FOURTEEN

The silent cheer leader.....

This section is dedicated to a person, who is not mentioned that often in this book. Yes, it's my father.

If you recall, in the previous incidents when I was under-confident and not reading, I have often mentioned my mother, who was tensed and making schemes for my betterment. That does not mean that my father was not concerned about me. He handled the situation very patiently. He firmly believed that may it be not today, but one day I would be able to read. It was just matter of time and I had to self inspired myself. He took immense efforts to ensure that I had enough opportunities to do so, sending me to Japan was one of those efforts. I can conclude that he created a suitable atmosphere for my mother to do her job.

My father also has a big hand in transitioning me from reading fantasy to exploring different genres. He introduced me to books related to finance, self help, career planning and some all time classics. Dear *baba* (father) thank you for giving flight to my reading journey.

CHAPTER FIFTEEN

When life paused.

By now 6th grade was over and covid-19 had entered our lives. We were put into lockdown. Let me surprise you, my lockdown wasn't boring. All thanks to reading.

Finally time wasn't a barrier to my reading. I could read as much as I wanted and whenever I wanted. There was nothing stopping me. Once I picked my 'Kindle' up, I used to sit in same state for next 3 to 4 hours.

Everything seemed perfect, but you might have noticed that since the start, my focus was inclined to English reading. It wasn't sufficient. As a citizen of Maharashtra I also had to ace Marathi reading.

Our neighbors, who as I mentioned earlier were closest to us both in terms of distance and relation, help me through it. That is Ketaki *tai* (elder sister), chinmayee *tai* (elder sister) and their mother 'pa'. This word 'pa' has story behind it too. I visited them since I was an infant and couldn't say her full name as 'Shilpa' so I ended up calling her 'Pa' and I still call her 'Pa'. They invested their precious time in fine tuning my Marathi, which always proves to be an asset to me. They introduced me to Marathi literature and other cultural aspects. So along with my regular reading this continued as well.

During lockdown I participated in various online elocution competitions. The toughest one was on '*Swatantraya veer Savarkar*' (freedom fighter Savarkar). The preparation started from researching and reading about this magnificent personality. I feel that my speech on '*Swatantraya veer Savarkar*' (freedom fighter Savarkar) has been my best piece of work until now. Even though I didn't win the competition, I gained a lot of information which otherwise I would have not.

What I am trying to prove here is that if I was inefficient with reading, I would not have participated because I wouldn't have been able to do the research necessary for it. This is the power of reading.

CHAPTER SIXTEEN

For readers-Recommended Reading

I read a lot in lockdown. To be precise 125 books ranging from 50 pages to 800 pages in various fonts. So let me list the best books, in my opinion, since I started reading.

1. Harry Potter (7 books) by J.K.Rowling
2. Percy Jackson and the Olympians (5 books) by Rick Riordan
3. Heroes of Olympus (6 books) by Rick Riordan
4. 0 to 1 by Peter Thiel, Blake Masters
5. Rich Dad Poor Dad by Robert Kiyosaki
6. How To Win Friends and Influence People by Dale Carnegie
7. How To Talk To Anyone by Leil Lowndes
8. The Topper Prepares by Soum Paul
9. *Mantra Shrimanticha* by Shyam Bhurke
10. Series Of Unfortunate Events (13 books) by Daniel Handler
11. Land of Stories (8 books) by Chris Colfer
12. 13 Reasons Why by Jay Asher
13. Romancing the Balance Sheet by Anil Lamba
14. Wise And Otherwise by Sudha Murti

15. Here There and Everywhere by Sudha Murti
16. Ikigai by Hector Garcia & Francesc Miralles

The earlier you read these books the more helpful they will prove to be. The fantasy ones will make you love reading and show you different styles of writing. The finance and self help ones will enhance your personality and teach you what schools don't teach. The books written on real incidences or people will widen your knowledge.

CHAPTER SEVENTEEN

For readers- How to start?

Now you have heard a lot about me. Let's talk about you dear readers. I hope you have been inspired by this book. So if you are inspired that means you want to start your extraordinary reading journey. Congratulations dear readers being inspired is the first step of starting this adventure.

Through my own experience, I have listed down one of the best ways of starting your reading journey!

1. Being inspired is the first step which we have already achieved.

2. Start with small books so they will end quickly and you will have the satisfaction of finishing a book, which will keep you enthusiastic throughout the journey.

3. Choose topics that you love because then your bigger focus will be on learning about your favourite topics and not on reading.

4. Start with languages you are comfortable with.

5. Read aloud, it will be like reading out to yourself and the chances of you getting bored will be cut down.

6. At the start reading daily can be difficult so set a fixed time for reading. May be 10 minutes, 20 minutes or two

pages, one chapter depending on the book you choose.

7. Eventually try replacing your screen time with reading.

8. Try using new words and phrases learned, in your day to day life. This will make you feel like you are using your time wisely and will sharpen your language.

CHAPTER EIGHTEEN

For readers - Benefits

1. The best benefit of reading is that it can act as an ice breaker. Basically, when you meet new people can start conversations regarding reading. Or, if you enter a new group of people no matter what they are speaking about, you will at least have some idea about the topic and can relate to it. You won't have fear of missing out.

2. Reading increases your focus and concentration which proves to be helpful in studies.

3. Your command on language will be exceptional.

4. As you will be acquiring a skill of reading you will gain confidence in yourself.

So, thank you dear readers for staying with me till the end of this book and hearing me out. Good luck for your reading journey.

If I could do it you definitely can!!!

9 798887 171210

Printed by Libri Plureos GmbH in Hamburg, Germany